Flying with Chinese

KB Student Book

Shuhan C. Wang, Ph. D. • **Carol Ann Dahlberg, Ph. D.**
Chiachyi Chiu, M.A. • Marisa Fang, M.S. • Mei-Ju Hwang, Ed.D.

© 2007 Marshall Cavendish International (Singapore) Private Limited

Published by Marshall Cavendish Education
A member of Times Publishing Limited
Times Centre, 1 New Industrial Road, Singapore 536196
Customer Service Hotline: (65) 6411 0820
E-mail: fps@sg.marshallcavendish.com
Website: www.marshallcavendish.com/education/sg

Distributed in North America by:

Cheng & Tsui Company,
25 West St, Boston, MA 02111
www.cheng-tsui.com
Toll Free 1-800-554-1963

First published 2007

All rights reserved. No part of this publication may be reproduced, stored in a retrieval system or transmitted, in any form or by any means, electronic, mechanical, photocopying, recording or otherwise, without the prior permission of the copyright owner.

ISBN 978-981-01-6675-5

Publisher: Lim Geok Leng
Editors: Yvonne Lee   Richard Soh   Rita Teng   Jo Chiu   Hu Jingping   Chong Liping
Chief Designer: Roy Foo

Printed by Times Graphics Pte Ltd

Preface

Flying with Chinese is a series designed to make the most of children's natural ability to learn language by creating meaningful contexts for learning and guiding them towards language proficiency, literacy development and cultural appreciation. Each book is based on a theme and integrated with other subject areas in the elementary school curriculum.

Flying with Chinese is standards-based and focuses on learners' performance. Some of the important elements in this series include the following:
1. Thematic planning and instruction, with emphasis on the principles and structure of a good story;
2. "Standards for Chinese Language Learning," which is part of the *Standards for Foreign Language Learning in the 21st Century*;
3. Principles of *Understanding by Design*;
4. Matching languages with children (*Languages and Children: Making the Match*).

Under three umbrella themes, each book in the series takes on a different but related sub-theme. These themes are interesting to the learners, connect with the curriculum of the elementary school, promote understanding of Chinese culture, and provide a context for language use.

The Student Book provides the basic story for the lessons, while the Workbook gives learners the opportunity to practice the language and use the concepts presented in the Student Book. The Teacher Guide suggests activities for each day and indicates when the Workbook pages are to be used.

Flying with Chinese focuses on a group of children who are learning Chinese together. These children and their families came from a wide range of backgrounds, and several are heritage Chinese speakers. One member of the group goes to China with her family, where she attends a Chinese school and shares her experiences with her former classmates. Throughout the series learners are introduced to legends, real and fictional characters of importance to Chinese culture, and significant customs, celebrations, and other elements of the Chinese way of life.

Flying with Chinese can be used independently or as part of a sequence of study in a program. Just as a child can fly a kite on his own or in a group, we hope that children will have fun flying these Chinese kites while gaining insight into the Chinese-speaking world.

我的朋友平平
My Friend Pingping

目录 Contents

Lesson 1	我和平平 Pingping and I	1
Lesson 2	平平有什么？What Does Pingping Have?	6
Lesson 3	春天来了 Here Comes Spring	11
Lesson 4	平平不见了！Pingping Is Missing!	17
Lesson 5	夏天来了 Here Comes Summer	23
Lesson 6	平平，你出来呀！ Pingping, Please Come Out to Play!	29
Lesson 7	秋天来了 Here Comes Fall	34
Lesson 8	平平在做什么呢？What Is Pingping Doing?	39
Lesson 9	冬天来了 Here Comes Winter	44
Lesson 10	下雪了 It's Snowing!	49
Lesson 11	我们大了一岁！ Pingping and I Are One Year Older!	55
Lesson 12	大家一起来！（评估） Let's Do It! (Performance Assessment Tasks)	62

第1课 我和平平

这是我。
我叫王大永。
我五岁。

我会读 五

我 会 认

I can do these things in Chinese, can you?

I can...
- tell who I am and who my friend is（我是……）
- tell how old I am or my friend is（我五岁）
- identify a zoo
- recognize the *hanzi* "友", know what it means and how to say it

第2课　平平有什么？

我有眼睛，也有耳朵。

我会读：耳

平平有什么？

我会读 有

I can...

- ❖ name the parts of my, my friend's, or my pet's face
- ❖ tell my friend that he or she is cute（可爱）
- ❖ tell people what I have（我有……）
- ❖ sing the song "我是大永" with the class
- ❖ recognize the *hanzi* "耳", know what it means and how to say it

第3课 春天来了

春天来了，常常下雨，天气不冷也不热。

我会读 春

我会念

春晓
孟浩然

春眠不觉晓，
处处闻啼鸟。
夜来风雨声，
花落知多少。

I can...
- talk about the weather in spring
- use my nose to smell （闻）
- use my ears to hear （听）
- recite the poem "春晓" with the class
- recognize the *hanzi* "雨", know what it means and how to say it

第4课 平平不见了！

春天，我去动物园看平平。

我会读 去

I can...
- ❖ ask where my friends are （在哪里？）
- ❖ tell "I'm here!" （在这里）
- ❖ tell "I like…" （喜欢）
- ❖ recognize the *hanzi* "不", know what it means and how to say it

我会唱

妹妹背着洋娃娃

妹妹背着 洋娃娃，

走到花园 来看花。

娃娃哭了 叫妈妈，

树上小鸟 笑哈哈。

我会认

I can do these things in Chinese, can you?

I can...
- talk about the weather in summer
- tell someone how I feel about summer
- sing the song "妹妹背着洋娃娃" with the class
- recognize the *hanzi* "鸟", know what it means and how to say it

第6课 平平，你出来呀！

我会读 躲

I can...
- ask a friend to come out to play
- ask my friends if they are hungry
- tell I like to do something (blow bubbles, eat something, play with water, sing a song)
- recognize the *hanzi* "竹", know what it means and how to say it

第7课　秋天来了

秋天来了，天空好蓝好蓝。

我会读　秋

可是平平还是只有白色和黑色。

我会读  白

彩虹歌

一 二 三 四　　五 六 七,

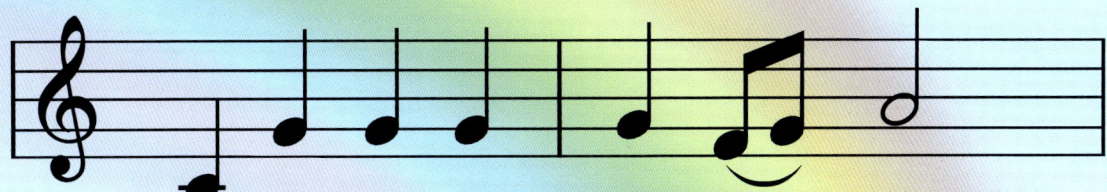

赤 橙 黄 绿　青　蓝 紫。

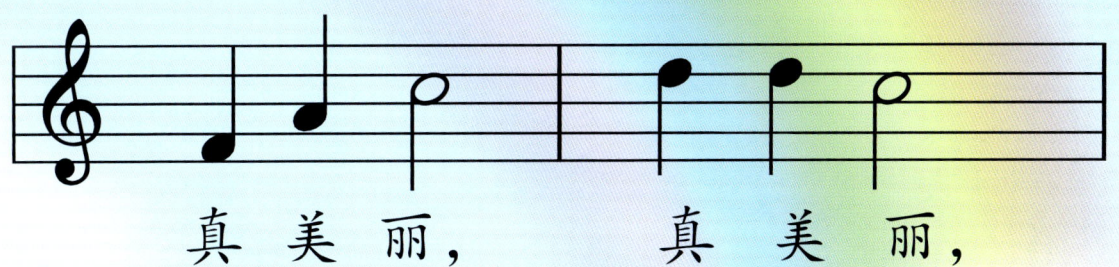

真 美 丽,　　真 美 丽,

七 色 彩 虹　真 美 丽。

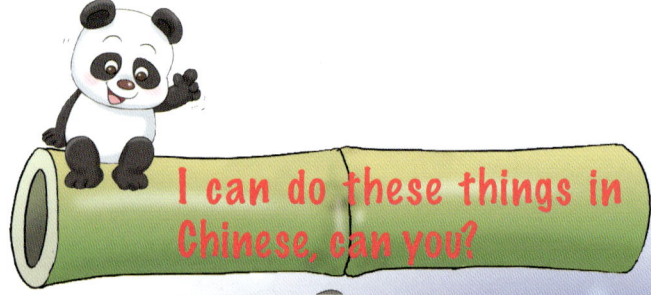

I can...
- ❖ tell that fall arrives （秋天来了）
- ❖ name some colors of the sky, leaves, rainbow and a panda
- ❖ tell someone my favorite colors
- ❖ sing the song "彩虹歌" with the class
- ❖ recognize the hanzi "白", know what it means and how to say it

第8课 平平在做什么呢?

秋天来了,天气好凉好凉。

我会读 凉

平平喜欢秋天。
我也喜欢秋天。

我会读 欢

我会认

I can do these things in Chinese, can you?

I can...
- tell someone about the weather in fall
- ask my friends to have fun with me, such as playing in the leaves, eating apples, playing with water, blowing bubbles, etc. （我们来……）
- recognize the *hanzi* "子", know what it means and how to say it

第9课 冬天来了

冬天来了,天气好冷好冷。

我会读 冬

它有厚毛皮,它不怕冷。它不用穿大衣。

我会读  毛

我没有厚毛皮,我怕冷。我要穿大衣。

我会读　衣

I can...
- ❖ talk about the weather in winter
- ❖ ask my friends if they are cold
- ❖ tell someone what I wear when I go outside to play
- ❖ tell someone how I feel about hot or cold weather
- ❖ recognize the *hanzi* "毛", know what it means and how to say it

我们玩得很高兴。

我会读 玩

平平喜欢冬天,我也喜欢冬天。

我会读  天

大熊猫

大熊猫,毛茸茸,
黑眼睛,黑耳朵,
还有一个大白脸。
爱爬树,爱玩水,
爱滑雪,爱睡觉,
还最喜欢吃绿竹。

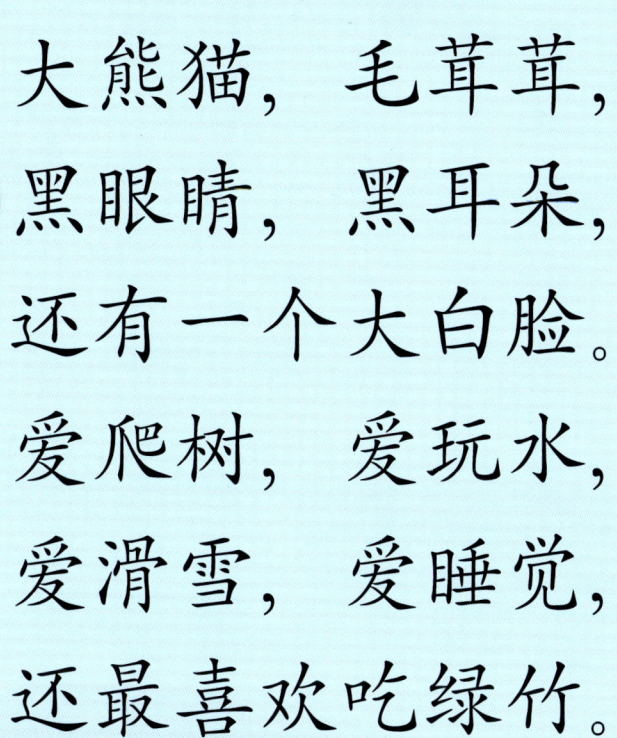

I can do these things in Chinese, can you?

I can...
- tell it is snowing
- tell someone what I like to do in the snow
- say the rhyme "大熊猫" with the class
- recognize the *hanzi* "天", know what it means and how to say it

第11课 我们大了一岁！

我会读：暖

春夏秋冬过一年。

我会读　年

我会读　听

平平大了一岁,
我也大了一岁。

我会读 岁

大一岁

春天到，放风筝，
夏天到，去游泳。
秋天到，采苹果，
冬天到，堆雪人。
春夏秋冬过一年，
你和我又大一岁。

我会认

友 耳 雨 不 鸟 子 竹 毛 白 天

I can do these things in Chinese, can you?

I can...
- tell that I'm one year older
- tell the four seasons of a year
- tell at least two parts of my face and what they can do
- say the rhyme "大一岁" with the class
- recognize the 10 hanzi that I learned in this book, know what they mean and how to say them

第12课　大家一起来！

汉字表
Hanzi List

耳
不
竹
子
天

友
雨
鸟
白
毛

词汇表
Vocabulary List

Hanzi	Pinyin	English	Page
Lesson 1			
王	Wáng	(a last name here)	1
大永	Dàyǒng	(a first name here)	1
五	wǔ	five	1
岁	suì	… years old	1
熊猫	xióng māo	panda	2
平平	Píngping	(a name here)	2
四	sì	four	2
住	zhù	live in	3
动物园	dòng wù yuán	zoo	3
好朋友	hǎo péng you	good friends	4
Lesson 2			
有	yǒu	have / has	6
眼睛	yǎn jing	eye	6

Hanzi	Pinyin	English	Page
耳朵	ěr duo	ear	6
鼻子	bí zi	nose	7
嘴巴	zuǐ ba	mouth	7

Lesson 3

Hanzi	Pinyin	English	Page
春天	chūn tiān	spring	11
常常	cháng cháng	often	11
下雨	xià yǔ	raining	11
天气	tiān qì	weather	11
冷	lěng	cold	11
热	rè	hot	11
花	huā	flower	12
开	kāi	bloom / open	12
鸟	niǎo	bird	12
叫	jiào	chirp / call	12
闻	wén	smell	13
花香	huā xiāng	fragrance of flowers	13
听	tīng	listen	13

Hanzi	Pinyin	English	Page
热闹	rè nao	hustle and bustle	14
Lesson 4			
不见了	bú jiàn le	disappear / missing	18
树上	shù shang	on the tree	19
躲	duǒ	hide	20
花丛	huā cóng	shrubs	20
喜欢	xǐ huan	like	21
Lesson 5			
夏天	xià tiān	summer	23
怕	pà	be afraid of	26
不喜欢	bù xǐ huan	dislike	26
躲起来	duǒ qi lai	hide	26
Lesson 6			
出来	chū lai	come out	30
吹泡泡	chuī pào pao	blow bubbles	30
竹子	zhú zi	bamboo	31
玩水	wán shuǐ	play with water	32

Hanzi	Pinyin	English	Page
Lesson 7			
秋天	qiū tiān	autumn, fall	34
天空	tiān kōng	sky	34
蓝	lán	blue	34
树叶	shù yè	leaf	35
颜色	yán sè	color	35
红色	hóng sè	red	35
橙色	chéng sè	orange	35
黄色	huáng sè	yellow	35
绿色	lǜ sè	green	35
可是	kě shì	but	36
还是	hái shi	still	36
只有	zhǐ yǒu	only have	36
白色	bái sè	white	36
和	hé	and	36
黑色	hēi sè	black	36

Hanzi	Pinyin	English	Page
Lesson 8			
凉	liáng	cool	39
苹果	píng guǒ	apple	41
熟了	shú le	ripen	41
叶子	yè zi	leaf	41
掉了	diào le	fallen	41
落叶	luò yè	fallen leaves	41
Lesson 9			
冬天	dōng tiān	winter	44
下雪	xià xuě	snowing	45
厚	hòu	thick	46
毛皮	máo pí	fur	46
不怕	bú pà	be not afraid of	46
不用	bú yòng	do / does not need	46
穿	chuān	wear	46
大衣	dà yī	coat	46

Hanzi	Pinyin	English	Page
Lesson 10			
堆	duī	pile	50
雪人	xuě rén	snowman	50
滑雪	huá xuě	ski	50
高兴	gāo xìng	happy	51
Lesson 11			
暖	nuǎn	warm	55
过	guò	pass	56
一年	yì nián	a year	56
声音	shēng yīn	sound	57
味道	wèi dào	taste / fragrance	58
一岁	yí suì	one year old	59

I can...

1. introduce myself and others ☐

2. tell my friend and I (we) are good friends ☐

3. tell the parts of my face and what they can do ☐

4. name the four seasons and tell the weather of a season ☐

5. tell what I can see, hear, smell, or touch in spring, summer, fall, or winter ☐

6. tell what I like or dislike ☐

7. ask my friend to have fun with me such as blowing bubbles, playing in the leaves, playing with water, making a snowman, or skiing in the snow ☐

8. name different colors and tell about my favorite colors ☐

9. tell something about a panda, such as where he lives, what he looks like, which season he likes or dislikes, what he likes to eat, and what he can do ☐

10. recite a Chinese poem, sing some Chinese songs, and chant some Chinese rhymes ☐